Jobs if You Like...

Music

Charlotte Guillain

Heinemann
LIBRARY
Chicago, Illinois

H www.capstonepub.com
Visit our website to find out more information about Heinemann-Raintree books.

To order:
☎ Phone 800-747-4992
🖳 Visit www.capstonepub.com
to browse our catalog and order online.

Edited by Rebecca Rissman, Daniel Nunn, and Adrian Vigliano
Designed by Steve Mead
Picture research by Mica Brancic
Originated by Capstone Global Library
Printed and bound in China

16 15 14 13
10 9 8 7 6 5 4 3 2

Library of Congress Cataloging-in-Publication Data
Guillain, Charlotte.
  Music / Charlotte Guillain.
    p. cm.—(Jobs if you like...)
  Includes bibliographical references and index.
  ISBN 978-1-4329-6809-0 (hb)—ISBN 978-1-4329-6820-5 (pb) 1. Music—Vocational guidance—Juvenile literature. I. Title.
  ML3795.G95 2013
  780.23—dc23   2011031929

Acknowledgments
We would like to thank the following for permission to reproduce photographs: Alamy pp. 27 (© ABN Images), 10 (© Chris Fredriksson), 8 (© David R. Frazier Photolibrary, Inc.), 5 (© GerryRousseau), 22 (© RichardBaker), 26 (© Stefan Sollfors), 12 (© Ahowden); Getty Images pp. 18 (Blend Images/Inti St Clair), 25 (Cultura/moodboard), 13 (Kevin Winter), 21 (McClatchy-Tribune/Fort Worth Star-Telegram), 20 (the Agency Collection. Credit: Chris Schmidt); Glow Images pp. 4 (Beyond/Lisa Penn), 7 (Blend RM/Hill Street Studios), 6 (Corbis/© James L. Amos), 17 (Corbis/Veer/© Fancy), 24 (Hana / Imagenavi), 9 (Hana/Imagenavi), 15 (Imagebroker), 11 (Stock Connection/Lucidio Studio, Inc.); Shutterstock pp. 16 (© Anton Gvozdikov), 14 (© Faraways), 19 (© Kzenon), 23 (© Susan Quinland-Stringer).

Cover photo of a young male DJ playing records at nightclub reproduced with permission of Getty Images (Stone/Paul Bradbury).

Every effort has been made to contact copyright holders of material reproduced in this book. Any omissions will be rectified in subsequent printings if notice is given to the publisher.

Contents

Some words are shown in bold, **like this**. You can find out what they mean by looking in the glossary.

Why Does Music Matter?

Do you play a musical instrument or enjoy singing? Or maybe you just love listening to music? Music is all around us every day, on the radio, on television, and on the Internet.

Music is an important part of many people's lives.

People play amazing music in all kinds of places.

We listen to music to relax, to dance, and to make us happy! It's fun to play and sing with other people and **entertain** an audience. There are many different jobs that involve music in all sorts of ways. Read on to find out more!

Be a Music Therapist

Does music sometimes change the way you feel? If you were a music **therapist**, you would use music to help people to feel better. You might cheer people up by helping them play instruments or sing together.

Many music therapists work with disabled children.

Music therapists can use music to make people happier.

Music therapists need to know how to play musical instruments very well. They also need to be good at talking and listening to people. They enjoy helping people have fun by making music.

7

Be a Sound Engineer

If you like working with gadgets and **equipment**, then maybe you could be a sound **engineer**. Sound engineers work in a **recording studio**, using equipment to record music and other sounds for radio, film, television, and Websites.

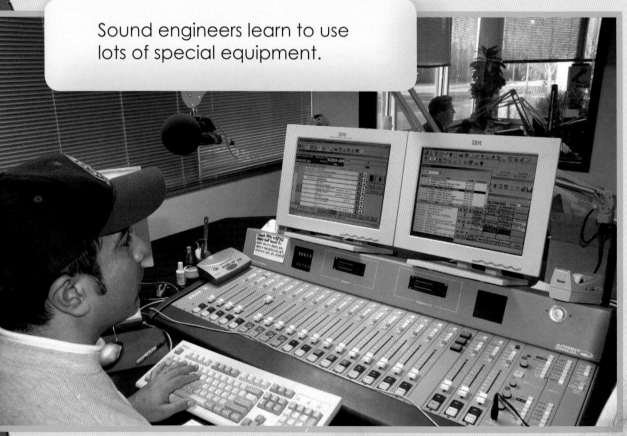

Sound engineers learn to use lots of special equipment.

Sound engineers need to know about different types of music. They need to be able to hear very well and have a good sense of **rhythm**. They work with different people all the time.

Sound engineers help musicians make the best sound as they play.

Be a Composer

If you like making up your own music and songs, then you could be a **composer**. Composers can write music for orchestras or rock bands. Some composers write music for advertisements or computer games.

Many composers include lots of different instruments in their music.

Composers are usually very good musicians and enjoy playing music. Sometimes they use computers to help them write new music. It can take a long time to write a new piece of music.

Composers experiment with different sounds as they write new music.

Be a Musical Agent

If you were a musical agent, you would listen to lots of singers and musicians. You might find them on the Internet. You would find the best **performers** and help them to get work. You might help someone become a star!

All sorts of musicians work with musical agents.

Singers and musicians need agents to help them make the right choices.

Musical agents need to be able to spot the best performers. They help their **clients** by organizing their work. They help singers and musicians decide where to work and what songs to perform.

Be a Professional Musician

If you are very good at playing an instrument or singing, then maybe you could be a professional musician. You might play in live concerts with an orchestra. You could make recordings for people to listen to on the radio or television, or to download.

Only the best musicians can play in a professional orchestra.

Professional musicians spend a lot of time learning and practicing new pieces of music. They need to take good care of their instrument or voice. They work in new places and with different people all the time.

Many professional musicians work in theater.

Be a Performing Artist

If you were a performing artist, you would work hard recording and performing songs. You might write your own songs or play songs your manager chooses. Often bands and singers are only popular for a short time.

Some performing artists get to make music for huge crowds of people!

Session musicians enjoy working with many different people.

Session musicians play with different bands when they need extra musicians. They can work with lots of great bands and singers. They are usually very talented musicians who can play many different musical styles.

Be a DJ

If you were a DJ, you might play music and talk on the radio. Other DJs play music for people to dance to in clubs. You would need to know a lot about music and choose the best songs for the people listening.

Radio DJs work in a studio with lots of special equipment.

DJs need to know how to use lots of different **equipment**. Sometimes they make their own sounds and add effects to the music. They need to have plenty of energy and a good sense of **timing**.

DJ is short for disc jockey.

Be a Promotions Manager

Are you good at talking to people? Maybe you could be a promotions manager. It would be your job to tell people about a band or orchestra's music and concerts. You would talk to **journalists** about the musicians.

Promotions managers make sure everyone knows about a new song or concert.

It's important for bands to be on television to tell people what they are doing.

Promotions managers sometimes work for a record company. They might arrange **photo shoots** for a singer or band. They try to get their musicians on television or in newspapers.

Be Backstage Crew

If you like traveling and listening to live music, then you could be part of a band's backstage crew. You would help to set up concerts and other events. You might set up musical instruments or organize the sound or lighting **equipment** for a concert.

The backstage crew who set up the stage are called "roadies."

The backstage crew have to pack the equipment away carefully after a show. It is hard work, with lots of late nights and traveling. But the crew see lots of bands playing live!

The backstage crew make sure everything is working properly during a show.

Be a Music Producer

If you were a music producer, your job would be to arrange the recording of a band's songs. You might help a new band record a demo so that they can sell a song to a record company.

Music producers talk to a band about how to make their music sound better.

Music producers often choose the sound **engineers** and studio for a recording. They might suggest changes to the music or **lyrics** of a song. They help choose which songs to include on a band's new album.

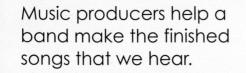

Music producers help a band make the finished songs that we hear.

Choosing the Right Job for You

When you decide what you want to do when you grow up, don't just think about school subjects. Think about what you enjoy doing. If you don't want to work late at night, then you wouldn't like being backstage crew!

If you are very good at playing music or singing, then you might be able to perform. It isn't easy, and very few people do this for a living. But there are many other interesting musical jobs, and there should be something to suit everyone.

Five things you couldn't do without music

- Dance
- Go to concerts
- Enjoy exciting films
- Learn to play an instrument
- Sing

27

Music Job Chart

If you want to find out more about any of the jobs in this book, start here:

	Backstage crew	Composer	DJ	Music producer	
You need to:	Be strong and hardworking	Have lots of ideas for new music	Know a lot about music and bands	Be good at explaining your ideas	
Best thing about it:	Listening to great live music!	Hearing people play your music!	People dancing to your music!	Seeing your recording top the charts!	

Music therapist	Popular musician	Professional musician	Promotions manager	Sound engineer	Musical agent
Be able to play several instruments	Be very determined	Be very good at playing an instrument or singing	Be good at talking to people	Be able to hear different sounds	Go to lots of concerts and listen to lots of bands
Making people happy!	Having a number-one song!	Hearing the audience clap!	Seeing your band on television!	Making a song sound fantastic!	Finding a new star!

Glossary

client person who pays another person to work for them

composer person who writes new pieces of music

engineer person who uses science and math to make tools, buildings, and machines

entertain show an audience something interesting

equipment something made to be used in a special way

journalist person whose job is to collect news and information and share it with people on television, radio, and in newspapers

lyrics words to a song

performer person who sings, dances, or acts for an audience

photo shoot session where a photographer takes a lot of photos of people

recording studio special place where music is recorded

rhythm regular sound pattern

session musician musician who sings or plays instruments with bands for recordings or performances

therapist person who is trained to help people using special treatment

timing knowing when to do something

Find Out More

Music Jobs

www.bls.gov/k12/music.htm

If you love music, this Website will give you some ideas for jobs using music and more information about them. If you don't understand some of the information, ask an adult for help.

San Francisco Symphony

www.sfskids.org/templates/home.asp?pageid=1

You can find out more about the instruments in an orchestra on this Website of the San Francisco Symphony. You can also experiment with the different sounds of music.

Playmusic.org

www.playmusic.org

On this Website you will find more information about a job in music. You will also find interviews with people who work in and with orchestras.

Index